Questions to Change Your Life

Questions to Change Your Life

A Self-Reflection Book

Melissa Lashyn

Published by Tablo

Table of Contents

This book is dedicated to

My beautiful, sweet mother, who was battling cancer while this book was written.

And my father, who has shown us all what true love really looks like.

And to all of you. For taking an exciting step in your growth journey by purchasing this book.

15% of profits generated from this book will be donated to organizations helping families impacted by cancer and other terminal illnesses. For an exact list of organizations that will receive funding, visit www.questionstochangeyourlife.com/impact.

Preface

"The only questions that matter are the questions you ask yourself." Ursula K Le Guin

"The quality of your life comes down to the quality of the questions you ask yourself on a daily basis." Tony Robbins

"The value you receive from reflective thinking will depend on the kinds of questions you ask yourself." John C Maxwell

The idea for this book started in 2019. The idea came, ironically exactly a month before what was next going to be the hardest six months of my entire life. As a self-motivated, driven individual, I had aspirations of writing a book that would help people visualize their grandest version of what their life could be, and then help them create a mindset that would allow them to accomplish this. I wanted to create a simple approach, using the questions we ask ourselves, to help people change the way they view themselves and their life at large. I knew that in so many ways, people limit themselves unknowingly simply by reacting to the programmed questions and thoughts they have wired in their minds. People will often ask themselves questions such as, "Why is life so hard?" or "Why does this keep happening to me?" when simply asking a different question such as, "What can I learn from this?" or others you will find in this book, can profoundly help frame a situation differently.

I know that helping people reframe their minds, using the questions we ask ourselves, can have profound impacts on how we view situations, the opportunities that might come our way, and ultimately dramatically change the trajectory of our lives. I knew this could happen because I have seen it happen time and time again with individuals on my teams and, giving a personal example, I have seen it with myself.

I began my adulthood in a marriage that wasn't a good fit for me. I realized I got married at a young age and before I had a chance to understand what was really important to me. And although we were both good people, we did not bring out the best in each other and it, unfortunately, turned into a very negative relationship. Because of this, and because of many toxic thought patterns I had, I was clinically anxious and experienced several painful years with chronic insomnia. The months of my insomnia had to be some of the darkest months of my life. Not only was I struggling with panic attacks from my mind racing about the potential of getting a divorce, I was also worrying about finances as it was hard for my husband at the time to find steady work in his field. I also became so anxious about not being able to sleep, I developed performance anxiety where I would become nervous about having another sleepless night that I would begin to be anxious about sleeping before bedtime. Being anxious about sleeping ended up creating more insomnia and thus I created a terrible, perpetual loop of anxiety and insomnia for myself. I felt like an absolute failure given that I could not do the one basic task every human in the world could do, which was fall asleep. This, coupled with a failing marriage and many toxic thought patterns left me feeling hopeless and defeated in every way.

I knew something had to change. I then began to learn from professionals such as therapists and sleep doctors, and focused on reframing my mind. Slowly and surely, I began to see progress. I then developed very strong, almost religious habits that involved asking myself specific questions before I went to bed and first thing in the morning. This habit helped me shift my mind, and change my behaviors from a toxic mindset to a healthy, growth mindset. It ultimately led me to a life I am not only proud of, but also feel fulfilled in almost every way. Moreover, I have developed a level of self-love and acceptance that I am proud of, considering how dark my mind was and how much I disliked, even hated, myself at one point. I have seen rich improvements in every area of my life and now I want to help others reach the same point of self-love, acceptance, and fulfillment in their own life.

Now, as I mentioned before, as I started writing this book, my life took a very difficult turn. During that time frame, my mother was diagnosed with stage 4 cancer. Despite this unfavorable diagnosis, my mom, being the incredible warrior she is, was determined to fight it. As such, we as a family began our battle against cancer.

During this time I was able to experience first hand how cancer is one of the hardest things a family and a person will ever go through. It is a time when almost every painful emotion is felt and nothing about the entire experience makes sense or seems fair. I had to watch someone I love be in tremendous pain and fear given that my mom was on bed rest for almost the entirety of her illness. Nothing in my life could have prepared me for this and all I wanted was to turn back time to the blissful period before this was my family's reality.

Being faced with the fact that this indeed was our reality, I knew the role I had to play in her life. I had to be strength and hope for my mom during the hardest period of her life. I knew that as painful as this was for me, I could reframe this situation and still choose to embrace each day with love and gratitude for our precious time together. I wanted to do that for my mom in order to give her the unconditional love and support she needed. By reframing my days and situations using specific questions and mantras, this season soon became filled with some of the most precious moments I have ever had with my mom. I had more energy and started seeing God's beautiful hand strongly at work. Despite everything going on, I realized I had so much to be thankful for. Making sure I prioritized my own mental health as well, I felt more balanced and able to face these challenges. Don't get me wrong, there were still very, *very* hard moments. But even in those moments, I knew I would make it through. I knew I could rely on the love and support in my life and I had the ability to see love so strongly present.

I didn't know that, as I was writing this book, I would be the one who would need it the most. Some of the questions in this book were used to comfort me during some very dark days, and have made a profound difference in the specific situation I described above. I knew that if it helped me, it could help a lot of other people too. This is what motivated me to finish this book and get it into your hands.

I am excited for the journey you are in store for. I am not sure where we are meeting each other and what your story has been up to this point; I just know that these simple tools can help you fundamentally change your life. This is my prayer and wish for you. This book will give you reflective questions that will help change your perspective, your thought patterns, and ultimately your life. It's one of the simplest, easiest tools that you can put to work immediately in order to see exciting changes in all areas of your life. As Wayne Dyer says, "If you change the way you look at things, the things you look at change." This book was created with the purpose of helping you find gratitude in all moments of life, create an empowering mindset, and move your life in a direction you have always dreamed of. I invite you for a soul-shaping journey where you view your life through the lens of gratitude, love, and growth.

I am also excited to share with you that 15% of the profits from this book will be donated to families and individuals impacted by cancer. By making the choice to work through your own personal growth and purchasing this book, you have also helped families that are going through one of their toughest journeys.

As you start this journey, please be in touch. I would love to hear your story and where this book ends up taking you. You can reach me and the community at www.questionstochangeyourlife.com or on Facebook and Instagram: @Questionstochangeyourlife. I look forward to connecting.

With love,

Melissa Lashyn

Introduction: The Journey

"Self-reflection entails asking yourself questions about your values, assessing your strengths and failures, thinking about your perceptions and interactions with others, and imagining where you want to take your life in the future."
Robert L. Rosen

What if changing the questions you ask yourself could profoundly change your life?

We are here to begin an exciting journey of self-reflection. Together we will explore brand new perspectives in order to positively change the way we view ourselves, our lives, and our circumstances. Whether you are going through a difficult time, trying to break repeated self-limiting behaviors, or working on being the absolute best version of yourself, this reflective book will help you.

As I mentioned before, I created this book after going through one of the most difficult times of my life, which was being a caregiver to my mom while she battled stage 4 cancer. I knew I needed to write this journal in order to share questions and thought patterns that have helped me find joy and hope in some of the darkest moments of my life.

What I have learned through the challenging times of my life, and what I want to share with you is, as Brian Tracy says, "you have within you right now, everything you need to deal with whatever the world can throw at you." This reflective book will provide you tools and questions that will help you dig within to find everything you need to create an incredible life for yourself. It is a journey of self-discovery and growth.

This book is not intended to be read in one sitting or to be completed from beginning to end. It is intended to be used once per day during your reflection time. It is also intended to be used in those moments when you need support. The moments when you feel your mind spinning and your emotions kicking in. In those moments, my hope is you find peace through the reflections in this book.

There are four different approaches to using this book. Ultimately, the choice and the options are yours. I recommend that you also use a separate note journal for your reflections. This way you can reuse questions and space is not limited.

Ways to work through this book:

1. #Questionstochangeyourlifechallenge: Join others as we work through the #questionstochangeyourlifechallenge. This is a 30-day challenge for personal reflection and growth. The challenge involves journalling twice per day every day for at least 15 minutes. Get social with us and post updates tagging @Questionstochangeyourlife.

2. In Community with friends: Use this book as part of a book club or accountability group in order to encourage your friends' personal growth and support them. Simply choose a section or amount of time for reflection and then come to the next meeting ready for a great discussion.

3. Specific Purpose: There might be a specific reason as to why you purchased this book. I invite you to dive into that section and start working through this book in that specific section.

4. Reflective and Meditative Style: This is the most casual approach to this journal. I recommend starting with the #questionstochangeyourlifechallenge before moving on to this approach. This reflective style is one where you set the pace and flow as to what serves you for how long and how often. Please do share as you progress, tagging @questionstochangeyourlife. I look forward to hearing about your journey.

Section 1: Owning the Day

"This is your moment. Own it." Oprah Winfrey

"This is a wonderful day. I've never seen this one before." Maya Angelou

This section focuses on reflective questions that will help you make the most out of your everyday moments. The questions are grouped together to allow for a bite-sized reflection time at the beginning and end of each day. As you use this section on a regular basis, notice how your days become a bit richer with gratitude, intention, and even accomplishments. For myself, I have also found that these precious reflection moments are some of my favorite moments of the day. I hope you find the same.

Note: It is recommended that you use a separate journal for this section, as it enables you to reflect on each question set more than once.

Beginning of the Day Reflections

Begin your day aligned to your goals and with a full heart with meaningful reflection time. Choose whichever section below serves you for the day.

A Day Beginning with Gratitude

What are five things I am grateful for?

_____

_____

_____

_____

_____

_____

_____

_____

What are the moments I am most looking forward to today?

_____

_____

_____

_____

_____

_____

_____

_____

How can I express gratitude today? Are there loving ways I can express gratitude to others today?

_____

_____

_____

_____

_____

_____

_____

_____

For my least favorite moments of the day, how can I look at these moments through the lens of gratitude?

_____

_____

_____

_____

_____

_____

_____

_____

A Day Beginning with Determination

What are one to three things I want to accomplish today? How would accomplishing these items make me feel?

_____

_____

_____

_____

_____

_____

_____

_____

Beginning today, what am I proud of myself for?

_____

_____

_____

_____

_____

_____

_____

How am I using this day to bring me closer to my goals and my purpose? _For more on exploring and understanding your purpose, visit Section 3: Inspiration and Purpose._

_____

_____

_____

_____

_____

_____

_____

_____

_____

_____

What energy and emotion do I want to bring to the day as I complete these tasks?

_____

_____

_____

_____

_____

_____

_____

_____

_____

A Day Beginning with Hope

Having hope as my outlook, what am I excited for today?

_____

_____

_____

_____

_____

_____

_____

_____

_____

If I bring the energy of hope and optimism to every situation I face today, what does this change about my day?

_____

_____

_____

_____

_____

_____

_____

_____

If I put the lens of hope and optimism on my day, how does it change how I respond and view the day ahead?

_____

_____

_____

_____

_____

_____

_____

_____

_____

A Day Beginning with Love and Compassion

What are five things I love about myself specifically today?

_____

_____

_____

_____

_____

_____

_____

_____

_____

Where are specific areas where love is very present in my life?

_____

_____

_____

_____

_____

_____

_____

_____

Envisioning my day to come, where is love most present? Where are there less obvious areas that are still full of love?

_____

_____

_____

_____

_____

_____

_____

_____

Envisioning this day to come, which specific areas can I intentionally bring compassion and grace?

_____

_____

_____

_____

_____

_____

_____

_____

_____

How do I want people to leave me feeling today?

_____

_____

_____

_____

_____

_____

_____

_____

A Day Beginning with Confidence

Being authentically myself, what am I bringing to the day that makes this world better?

_____

_____

_____

_____

_____

_____

_____

_____

Picturing myself as my true, authentic self living my purpose: How do
I picture myself moving throughout the day? How do I interact with
others? How do they react to me? How do I show up for particularly
challenging parts of my day?

_____

_____

_____

_____

_____

_____

_____

_____

_____

What are all the reasons why I need to show up confidently today? How
will the world benefit by me showing up as my best, authentic self?

_____

_____

_____

_____

_____

_____

_____

_____

_____

Thinking of my role models, and people that inspire me, and visualizing
them moving throughout the day in my place, what would they do
differently than me? What can I learn from this?

_____

_____

_____

_____

_____

_____

_____

_____

A Day Beginning with Strength

What internally drives me to live an incredible life?

_____

_____

_____

_____

_____

_____

_____

_____

What externally drives me to show up as my strongest self?

_____

_____

_____

_____

_____

_____

_____

_____

If I keep my answers to the previous question top of mind, how does this change how I go through today? In other words, how can I show up differently using my life purpose and my internal/external drivers as my motivation and strength?

_____

_____

_____

_____

_____

_____

_____

_____

Living in my strength, what are several small goals I can set for the day?

_____

_____

_____

_____

_____

_____

_____

What moments today might allow me to show my strength through being vulnerable?

_____

_____

_____

_____

_____

_____

_____

_____

A Day Beginning with Self-love and Acceptance

What are five things I love about myself?

_____

_____

_____

_____

_____

_____

_____

_____

Looking at my gifts, passions, and abilities, what makes me unique?

_____

_____

_____

_____

_____

_____

_____

Looking at today in particular, what specific things can I do to show myself self-love?

_____

_____

_____

_____

_____

_____

_____

_____

_____

How does being more loving and kind to myself benefit the world around me today?

_____

_____

_____

_____

_____

_____

_____

_____

_____

End of the Day Reflections

End your day with a peaceful mind and a full heart. Choose whichever section below serves you for ending the day.

Ending the Day Reflecting on Gratitude

What am I the most thankful for today?

_____

_____

_____

_____

_____

_____

_____

_____

Were there any parts of my day where I wasn't living in gratitude? What can I learn from this?

_____

_____

_____

_____

_____

_____

_____

_____

Ending the Day Reflecting on Determination

As I reflect on my day, what am I proud of myself for?

_____

_____

_____

_____

_____

_____

_____

_____

Was there anything in my day that distracted me from my goals? What can I do to help myself with this in the future?

_____

_____

_____

_____

_____

_____

_____

_____

_____

What do I want to accomplish tomorrow?

_____

_____

_____

_____

_____

_____

_____

_____

Ending the Day Reflecting on Hope

What were my favorite moments of the day?

_____

_____

_____

_____

_____

_____

_____

_____

Where was hope evident today?

_____

_____

_____

_____

_____

_____

_____

_____

_____

What am I looking forward to tomorrow or the rest of this week?

_____

_____

_____

_____

_____

_____

_____

_____

Ending the Day Reflecting on Love and Compassion

Where was love present today? Where were the unexpected areas where love showed up?

_____

_____

_____

_____

_____

_____

_____

_____

_____

Were there any points where love could be more present? What can I
learn from this for future days?

_____

_____

_____

_____

_____

_____

_____

_____

Ending the Day Reflecting on Confidence

What am I proud of myself for today?

_____

_____

_____

_____

_____

_____

_____

_____

Where did I show up as my authentic, confident self the most?

_____

_____

_____

_____

_____

_____

_____

_____

_____

What enabled me to be my true, confident self? How can I take this into future days?

_____

_____

_____

_____

_____

_____

_____

_____

Ending the Day Reflecting on Strength

Where was my strength evident today?

_____

_____

_____

_____

_____

_____

What did I learn from today?

_____

_____

_____

_____

_____

_____

_____

_____

_____

What next steps can I take to keep this momentum going?

_____

_____

_____

_____

_____

_____

_____

_____

Ending the Day Reflecting on Self-love and Acceptance

What were a few of my favorite moments of today?

_____

_____

_____

_____

_____

_____

_____

_____

What is one thing I learned about myself today?

_____

_____

_____

_____

_____

_____

_____

_____

How was I kind to myself today?

_____

_____

_____

_____

_____

_____

_____

_____

What were the growth opportunities from today in this area? What can I take away from today in order to keep on building on my progress?

_____

_____

_____

_____

_____

_____

_____

_____

Section 2: Everyday Inspiration

"I get inspiration from my everyday life." Hayao Miyazaki

"I think it's important to find the little things in everyday life that make you happy." Paula Cole

This next section includes reflection questions that will help you in your day to day life. The topics included are intended to help you get the most out of your everyday moments. I invite you to examine both topics that interest you and those that you are apprehensive about working through. For the topic or topics that are bringing you apprehension, sit with that discomfort, and see what they might be trying to tell you.

As you work through the questions, bring one or two of them with you as you go about your day. Reflecting on these questions continuously throughout the day will allow you to make this way of thinking a habitual thought pattern. This will in turn begin the process of rewiring your brain to look for the gratitude, love, courage, and compassion in your day.

Choose a topic that serves you and your reflection time, and enjoy.

Topics to choose from include:

Gratitude - for the past and for today
Self-love and Acceptance
Courage & Strength
Love and Compassion
Evaluating the mind and thoughts
Mindfulness and Living in the moment

Gratitude

"Acknowledging the good you already have in your life is the foundation for all abundance" Eckhart Tolle

Gratitude single-handedly has the power to change your life. If you take only one thing away from this book, let it be gratitude. According to research, there are multiple health and life benefits gained from the single practice of gratitude. Research shows that gratitude improves mental health, physical health, relationships, interpersonal skills, and increases happiness, among many other benefits.

This section is divided into two areas: Gratitude for the past, and Gratitude for the present. Being thankful for where you came from and thankful for where you are now are both important for a holistic gratitude approach. As you work through these questions, bring this focus of gratitude into every area of your life and see how your world begins to change.

Gratitude for the past

"Let us remember the past with gratitude, live the present with enthusiasm, and look forward to the future with confidence." Pope John Paul II

This next section focuses solely on reflecting on the past through the lens of gratitude. We cannot have a grateful present or future if we aren't thankful for where we have come from. For some, the past can contain painful moments that might not be resolved. If this is the case for you, I encourage you to also work through the section in this book focused on adversity, forgiveness, and healing.

In this section, look back at your story through the lens of gratitude, and watch how it will help you become more thankful for the person you are today.

Reflecting on my entire story, including all of the ups and downs, what am I grateful for in who my journey helped me become?

_____

_____

_____

_____

_____

_____

_____

_____

What are some life events or memories that, at the time I perhaps didn't recognize, but have taught me incredible life lessons?

_____

_____

_____

_____

_____

_____

_____

Who are five people I am eternally grateful for, and what would I say to them to thank them?

_____

_____

_____

_____

_____

_____

_____

_____

Places carry so many memories with the smells, the people that fill
or filled them, and the specific time-frame they encompass. Reflecting
back, what are three places that fill your heart with gratitude? *With every
place you think of, include some precious memories as well.*

_____

_____

_____

_____

_____

_____

_____

_____

_____

Reflecting on my past, why am I thankful to be living this exact life?
What do I love the most about being me and who I am as a person?

_____

_____

_____

_____

_____

_____

_____

_____

_____

What are a few of my most precious memories? How did they make my
life special?

_____

_____

_____

_____

_____

_____

_____

_____

_____

Moments not meant for me: In the words of Buddha, "In the end, only three things matter: How much you loved, how gently you lived, and how gracefully you let go of things not meant for you." What 'closed doors' am I most thankful for?

_____

_____

_____

_____

_____

_____

_____

_____

What has been an incredible, unexpected surprise in my life and why did it turn out to be a wonderful blessing?

_____

_____

_____

_____

_____

_____

_____

_____

Where are five areas that God/the universe has shown up in my life, either presently or in the past?

_____

_____

_____

_____

_____

_____

_____

_____

_____

If I were to write a letter to my younger self about all of the wonderful blessings that would be coming my way, what would I say? *Pick any age of your younger self that you feel would need this letter the most.*

_____

_____

_____

_____

_____

_____

_____

_____

_____

Gratitude for the present

"The miracle of gratitude is that it shifts your perception to such an extent that it changes the world you see." Dr. Robert Holden

The next section is focused on gratitude for the present. As you bring gratitude to every area of your life, watch how these areas begin to change in response to the new energy you are showing up with. I invite you to also observe your thought patterns as you go throughout your day, and notice when you are having a negative or unwanted thought pattern. In those moments, I invite you to come back to these questions on gratitude and reflect on what you are thankful for. Reframing your perspective as you go throughout the day will help you refocus your brain to see the positive in these situations and continue to reap the incredible benefits of gratitude.

What are five things I am thankful for today?

_____

_____

_____

_____

_____

_____

_____

_____

_____

What are 5-10 little moments in my day or week that I often overlook but are some of my favorite moments of the week?

_____

_____

_____

_____

_____

_____

_____

_____

_____

Gratitude in the chaos: Are there any chaotic, busy moments of my life, in which I can reframe with gratitude? To find a mantra focused on gratitude, visit www.questionstochangeyourlife.com/resources.

_____

_____

_____

_____

_____

_____

_____

_____

_____

For the next question, imagine if you were a time traveler. You have the gift of going back in time in order to enjoy some of your favorite days again. Now imagine you were from the future, and picked today to relive again. If I were from the future, and intentionally came back to live today, what would I be most thankful for? Why would I have chosen this exact day to visit?

_____

_____

_____

_____

_____

_____

_____

_____

_____

What are three areas of my life I can reframe from "I have to…" to "I get to…"?

_____

_____

_____

_____

_____

_____

_____

_____

_____

My body: What are three things I am thankful for with my physical body? What does it allow me to do or who does it allow me to become?

_____

_____

_____

_____

_____

_____

_____

_____

My mind: What are three things I am thankful for when reflecting on my mind and the vast amount of knowledge it holds. What does it allow me to do or who does it allow me to become?

_____

_____

_____

_____

_____

_____

_____

How does practicing gratitude allow me to be kinder and more loving to myself today?

_____

_____

_____

_____

_____

_____

_____

_____

_____

Maybe there are areas in my life where progress is not where I would like it to be. What are those areas and what can I still be grateful for?

_____

_____

_____

_____

_____

_____

_____

_____

Looking into the future with gratitude, what am I thankful in advance for? In other words, what am I thankful for in my future?

_____

_____

_____

_____

_____

_____

_____

_____

Other categories: I invite you to choose specific areas of your life to find gratitude. Simply choose a category below and write down all of the things you are thankful for in this area. There might be some categories that are harder to complete than others and specific areas you are less grateful in at this moment. I invite you to sit in this discomfort and reflect on it. See if there are any learnings through this process, and see where you can still find gratitude.

- Health:

_____

_____

_____

_____

_____

_____

_____

_____

_____

- Family: Immediate / Extended

_____

_____

_____

_____

_____

_____

_____

_____

_____

- Finances:

_____

_____

_____

_____

_____
_____
_____
_____
_____

- Romantic:

_____
_____
_____
_____
_____
_____
_____
_____

- Extracurricular activities:

_____
_____
_____
_____
_____
_____
_____
_____

- Residence: Country / City / Neighborhood

_____
_____
_____
_____

_____

_____

_____

_____

_____

- Vocation:

_____

_____

_____

_____

_____

_____

_____

_____

- Home:

_____

_____

_____

_____

_____

_____

_____

- Nature:

_____

_____

_____

_____

_____

_____

_____

_____

_____

-Other:

_____

_____

_____

_____

_____

_____

_____

_____

Self-love and Acceptance

"Your greatest responsibility is to love yourself and know you are enough."
Chetna Mishra

This next section focuses on creating a mindset around self-love and acceptance. The questions are intended to help you love and accept yourself as the unique masterpiece that you are. As you work through this section, also observe the day to day thoughts you have towards yourself. Specifically, observe the thoughts you have when you look at yourself in the mirror, or when you make a mistake. As you catch yourself thinking negative or unloving thoughts about yourself, I invite you to replace this thought pattern with a message of love, using one of the following questions.

Reflecting on the past, what are things I am proud of myself for?

_____

_____

_____

_____

_____

_____

_____

_____

_____

What are my natural abilities, or things that come easily for me?

_____

_____

_____

_____

_____

_____

_____

_____

What aspects of my character and personality traits make me unique?

_____

_____

_____

_____

_____

_____

_____

_____

What are my values? What are things that I stand for that I am proud of?

_____

_____

_____

_____

_____

_____

_____

_____

_____

What do I love about myself?

_____

_____

_____

_____

_____

_____

_____

_____

What do I need to forgive myself for?

_____

_____

_____

_____

_____

_____

_____

_____

What are all of the things I enjoy doing and that energize me? How can I add more of these items to my life?

_____
_____
_____
_____
_____
_____
_____
_____
_____

What can I do to love myself more, starting today?

_____
_____
_____
_____
_____
_____
_____
_____

What are things I should remove from my life in order to love myself
more? What things in my life aren't serving me?

_____
_____
_____
_____
_____
_____
_____
_____

How does increasing my self-love allow me to in turn love and support others more?

_____

_____

_____

_____

_____

_____

_____

_____

_____

Are there areas in my past (or currently) where I could have been kinder to myself? Using the lens of self-love and acceptance, what would I say to my younger self going through that difficult time?

_____

_____

_____

_____

_____

_____

_____

_____

_____

Are there any behaviors or habits I have that are based on insecurity or fear instead of love? What are other actions I can take in order to ensure I am being kind to myself?

_____

_____

_____

_____

_____

_____

_____

_____

_____

Courage and Strength

"Courage is not having the strength to go on; it's going on when you don't have the strength." Theodore Roosevelt

Moments that call us to be courageous often go on to define us in the future. Whether you are facing moments in the day where courage is needed, or a larger challenge in life, these reflection questions will help. As you go into moments when courage is needed, evaluate your thought patterns. Observing fear-based thought patterns and replacing them with thoughts of love, strength, and peace will get you one giant step closer to overcoming your fear and being courageous. Moments that call on us to be courageous are also showing us our growth opportunities in our lives. When fear hits, lean into these moments by reframing your mind to find the strength and motivation you have to overcome it. Remember, you have everything you need to succeed within you.

What inspires me to live my life to its fullest and be my strongest self? Who/What motivates me and gives me strength?

_____

_____

_____

_____

_____

_____

_____

_____

What character traits and values do I already possess that will serve me
during a time when courage is needed? Why can I lean on my character
traits and values to help give me confidence during this challenging
time?

_____

_____

_____

_____

_____

_____

_____

_____

_____

What purpose do I have that is bigger than myself? Why does my
purpose inspire me to show up in a courageous way?

_____

_____

_____

_____

_____

_____

_____

_____

What small steps can I take in order to start moving in a favorable
direction?

_____

_____

_____

_____

_____

_____

_____

_____

_____

Visualizing myself accomplishing my goals, what would I look like? How will I feel?

_____

_____

_____

_____

_____

_____

_____

_____

What am I overcoming through this?

_____

_____

_____

_____

_____

_____

_____

Are there people who have been on a similar path that I can reach out to for support?

_____

_____

_____

_____
_____
_____
_____
_____
_____
_____

Although some things can be very challenging to overcome, and there
still might be a significant journey ahead, what am I proud of myself for
accomplishing up to this point?

_____
_____
_____
_____
_____
_____
_____
_____
_____

What might be holding me back? How can I overcome this with love
and compassion for myself and others?

_____
_____
_____
_____
_____
_____
_____
_____
_____

Why will the world or others benefit from me living my best, truest,
authentic version of myself?

_____

_____

_____

_____

_____

_____

_____

_____

_____

How can I be more courageous by using vulnerability in my life?

_____

_____

_____

_____

_____

_____

_____

_____

What holds me back from being more vulnerable?

_____

_____

_____

_____

_____

_____

_____

_____

What are specific ways that showing a more vulnerable side would benefit my situation and / or overall life?

_____

_____

_____

_____

_____

_____

_____

_____

_____

_____

Love and Compassion

"You always gain by giving love." Reese Witherspoon

Aligning with love and compassion is one of the best ways to remove ego, pride, and fear from your life. This next section reflects on love and compassion and its abundant presence in your life. Living in love and compassion is how your true, authentic self is revealed. It creates a mindset of abundance over fear. As you work through this section, notice when your thoughts go to a place of fear or ego, and reflect on what you can learn about yourself through this. Use the questions below to help you identify and see the infinite love and compassion present in your life.

Where is love very present in my life? *List all of the different areas and people that surround you with love.*

_____

_____

_____

_____

_____

_____

_____

_____

_____

In which moments in my life have I felt the most loved? What did these moments teach me or help me to become?

_____

_____

_____

_____

_____

_____

_____

_____

What are some moments from my past where I could have been more compassionate with myself? When could I have shown more compassion towards others?

_____

_____

_____

_____

_____

_____

_____

_____

How can I intentionally create more moments filled with love in my life?

_____

_____

_____

_____

_____

_____

_____

_____

_____

How can I show up in my life with love and compassion?

_____

_____

_____

_____

_____

_____

_____

_____

How do I want people to feel when they interact with me?

_____

_____

_____

_____

_____

_____

_____

_____

How does my life transform if I act intentionally from a place of love?

_____

_____

_____

_____

_____

_____

_____

_____

_____

Where is fear and ego present in my life? What does this tell me about my core fears and needs?

_____

_____

_____

_____

_____

_____

_____

_____

_____

What would it look like to replace thoughts of fear or ego with love and compassion?

_____

_____

_____

_____

_____

_____

_____

_____

_____

What are simple things I can do to start putting love into action every day?

_____

_____

_____

_____

_____

_____

_____

_____

_____

If it's the little moments that make everyday special, how can I share or express more love through small acts throughout my day?

_____

_____

_____

_____

_____

_____

_____

_____

_____

Evaluating the Mind and Thoughts

"You either control your mind or it controls you." Napoleon Hill

The limit on your life is not the sky, or the moon, as many cliche sayings lead us to believe. The limit on your life is your mind and what you choose to believe and tell yourself every day. Use this section liberally in order to understand and remove the self-limiting beliefs your tell yourself. Everyone has self-limiting beliefs, however, not everyone is consciously aware of the limiting things they tell themselves. This section is intended to help you bring awareness to what you focus on and change your thinking pattern around thoughts that are not beneficial to you. As you go throughout the day, start observing your thought patterns, and use these questions to help reprogram your thinking.

When evaluating my thoughts, what are my recurring, self-limiting beliefs?

_____

_____

_____

_____

_____

_____

_____

_____

After writing all of my self-limiting beliefs (see previous question), what about them makes them un-true or not beneficial to me? What is a counter-argument for each of them?

_____

_____

_____

_____

_____

_____

_____

_____

When evaluating my thoughts throughout the day, what emotion(s) are they creating? Is this an emotion that is positive and serving me?

_____

_____

_____

_____

_____

_____

_____

_____

_____

Are there specific emotions I tend to gravitate towards (ie I tend to become angry, hurt or betrayed really easily)? What can I learn about myself through identifying these emotions I gravitate towards?

_____

_____

_____

_____

_____

_____

_____

Are there other times in my past I remember distinctly feeling these emotions or having these specific thoughts? What are some parallels or similarities I can draw between this situation and the last time(s) I felt this way?

_____

_____

_____

_____

_____

_____

_____

_____

What can I focus my attention on instead that would produce positive emotions and focus my energy in the direction I would like to go?

_____

_____

_____

_____

_____

_____

_____

_____

I invite you to now use the next section on mindfulness for tips on truly focusing on the now. Using self-love, I invite you to release your self-limiting thoughts and focus your mind back on the here and now and the positive emotions that serve you.

Mindfulness and Living in the Moment

"Do not lose yourself in the past. Do not lose yourself in the future. Do not get caught in your anger, worries, or fears. Come back to the present moment and touch life deeply. This is mindfulness." Thich Nhat Hanh

The present moment is where life happens and where all opportunities lie. The concept of mindfulness has gained popularity over the past few years given its cited health and wellness benefits. Mindfulness is the ability to be aware of and observe the present moment without reaction or judgment. It is used in many meditation practices as a way to reduce stress, gain control of one's thoughts, and improve overall well-being.

The purpose of this section is to help you become present in this exact moment. Use these questions before your meditation time or whenever you feel your mind wander or start to spin. Notice how bringing your thoughts back to the present moment and clearing your mind changes your mood and the busyness of your thoughts. For optimal results, I encourage a regular and consistent mindfulness meditation practice.

Note: Journal space is available for the section below, however in my practice I do not choose to write the answers down. Instead I choose to bring my awareness to them only.

External: What are five things I see, two things I hear, one thing I taste and one thing I smell?

_____

_____

_____

_____

_____

_____

_____

Internal: Bringing my awareness to my <u>feet</u>, what do the insides of my feet feel? Is there any tension that I am holding in this space? If yes, am I okay to release this tension? *Now repeat the question above multiple times, moving up your body and replacing 'feet' with the next body part until you have arrived at your head. The main areas to focus on are lower legs, upper legs, hips, stomach, chest, arms, neck, and head, and any other areas you feel are holding tension.*

_____

_____

_____

_____

_____

_____

_____

_____

Now let yourself go and live in this exact moment. Observe what emotions and thoughts arise, without any judgment on yourself or your thoughts. If there are painful, uncomfortable emotions you are experiencing, I invite you to continue to feel them and sit with them. Observe where it is showing up physically in your body and give yourself permission to lovingly release this tension. As you sit with these uncomfortable emotions, you will create the space for growth and release.

Section 3: Inspiration and Purpose

"Create the highest, grandest vision possible for your life, because you become what you believe." Oprah Winfrey

"Your only limit is your mind." Unknown

"Believe in your heart that you're meant to live a life full of passion, purpose, magic and miracles." Roy Bennett

Sometimes all we need to spark inspiration is simply a different perspective. The questions in this section are intended to provide you just that. Use the questions listed here as tools to help you unlock and identify the potential you know you have. This section will help you align with your true purpose, help give you clarity in decision making, and provide a different perspective for when you are feeling stuck.

Evaluating Purpose and Direction

This section could be a book topic of its own and there are great books that do a wonderful job helping people evaluate and discover their purpose and direction. The intention of this section is to provide you with thought-provoking questions that will help you refine and be confident in your purpose and direction of your life.

Gaining Inspiration from Reflecting on the Past

Reflecting on the past, what are 5-10 moments that really energized me and made me feel alive? *Think of a variety of different examples.*

_____

_____

_____

_____

_____

_____

_____

_____

_____

For every one of those moments:

- What was I doing?

_____

_____

_____

_____

_____

_____

_____

_____

- Why did I love it?

_____

_____

_____

_____

_____

_____

_____

_____

- What emotions was I experiencing during this time?

_____

_____

_____

_____

_____

_____

_____

- How was I making this world a better place?

_____

_____

_____

_____

_____

_____

_____

What are several ways I can create more of these moments in my life? *Tip: Brainstorm a list of at least 20 ways. It'll help you get more creative with the more ideas you challenge yourself to brainstorm.*

_____

_____

_____

_____

_____

_____

_____

_____

Gaining Inspiration from my Gifts, Talents, and Passions

What am I really good at? *People at times have a hard time acknowledging their strengths. During this exercise, I encourage you to list everything and celebrate your talents.*

_____

_____

_____

_____

_____

_____

_____

_____

What are the things I really enjoy doing? *Use your first list for reference, marking items you really enjoy, and then add any other items not included.*

_____

_____

_____

_____

_____

_____

_____

_____

What are my values? What do I deeply care about? *For reference, you can find a list of values at www.questionstochangeyourlife.com/resources.*

_____

_____

_____

_____

_____

_____

_____

_____

Reflecting on this list, what can I offer the world that is very unique to me, my skill sets, and passions?

_____

_____

_____

_____

_____

_____

_____

_____

How can I use these gifts, talents, and passions to serve others and make this world a better place?

_____

_____

_____

_____

_____

_____

_____

_____

Starting with today or this week, how can I make the most out of today using my gifts, talents, and passions?

_____

_____

_____

_____

_____

_____

_____

_____

_____

Gaining Inspiration from Creating my Perfect Day and Week

From start to finish, how would I describe my perfect day? How would I start my day? What activities would be involved?

_____

_____

_____

_____

_____

_____

_____

_____

What emotions would I experience as I move through my perfect day?

_____

_____

_____

_____

_____
_____
_____
_____
_____

Who would I spend my day with?

_____
_____
_____
_____
_____
_____
_____
_____

Expanding on my perfect day, what other items would I include to make it a perfect week?

_____
_____
_____
_____
_____
_____
_____

Reflecting on my perfect day and week described, what does this tell me about my ultimate goals?

_____
_____

_____

_____

_____

_____

_____

_____

_____

_____

- What does it tell me about what I value?

_____

_____

_____

_____

_____

_____

_____

_____

_____

- What does it tell me about how I ultimately want to feel?

_____

_____

_____

_____

_____

_____

_____

_____

_____

What are all of the things I tell myself that are stopping me from living this life now?

_____
_____
_____
_____
_____
_____
_____
_____

- For every point I made in the above question, what counterpoints can I make that make those statements simply untrue?

_____
_____
_____
_____
_____
_____
_____

What are small steps I can make in order to make my perfect day and week a reality?

_____
_____
_____
_____
_____
_____
_____

What are the dramatic steps can I take in order to make my perfect day
and week a reality?

_____

_____

_____

_____

_____

_____

_____

_____

_____

Alternatively, what am I filling my days with now that does not serve me
and my perfect day or week?

_____

_____

_____

_____

_____

_____

_____

_____

_____

Gaining Inspiration from Evaluating the Future and Other Perspectives

My legacy: When I think forward to the end of my life, what do I want
my legacy to be?

_____

_____

_____

_____

_____

_____

_____

_____

_____

What do I want to be written in my obituary?

_____

_____

_____

_____

_____

_____

_____

_____

What do I want those closest to me to think and say about me?

_____

_____

_____

_____

_____

_____

_____

_____

What would be my biggest regrets if I knew I only had a limited time left? How can I act on this sooner, starting with the items that are in my control?

_____

_____

_____

_____

_____

_____

_____

_____

_____

_____

If I were to have a conversation with myself as a child, what would my child self be proud of me for in my life at the moment? What is an area of my life that my child self would want me to change or improve?

_____

_____

_____

_____

_____

_____

_____

_____

_____

Gaining Inspiration from Focusing on Energy

This section is inspired by the law of attraction. The premise behind the law of attraction is that 'like attracts like' and therefore, you do not attract what you want, rather you attract what you are. The science behind this law states that in order to attract what you want, depends on how you feel towards it. The more feelings of gratitude and appreciation you have, the more you will attract. There are many great books written on this topic. I recommend reading more about this if it is new to you and something that interests you. This next section uses this as its foundation and focuses your reflection on what you want to feel. After this is understood, it then incorporates those feelings and visualizations into your everyday living.

When dreaming big about my life or my next step in my life, what do I visualize in my mind? What does my dream life look like?

_____

_____

_____

_____

_____

_____

_____

_____

_____

As I create these visualizations, what am I thinking/feeling/doing? *It is important when you are visualizing it, that you visualize yourself in first person as if you are living through it and the experience is happening to you.*

_____

_____

_____

_____

_____

_____

_____

_____

_____

Focusing on feelings only, what are the emotions I want to feel once this happens to me?

_____

_____

_____

_____

_____

_____

_____

_____

_____

What do I have overwhelming gratitude for when I visualize this?

_____

_____

_____

_____

_____

_____

_____

_____

When it is December 31st of this year, what do I want to look back and say I have accomplished? *Answer the same question with varying timeframes: two years, five years, ten years.*

_____

_____

_____

_____

_____

_____

_____

_____

Questions to Reflect on when Making a Major Life Decision

This book can't make your final decision for you; what it can do is help you evaluate different perspectives in order to feel confident that you have ultimately made the best decision for you. The following questions are intended to do just that.

When evaluating this decision, is the outcome in alignment with my overall purpose? How does each choice align with my overall purpose?

_____

_____

_____

_____

_____

_____

_____

_____

_____

Opportunity for growth: How will each scenario help me grow? Is there one scenario that helps me grow more and in areas I am looking for growth in?

_____

_____

_____

_____

_____

_____

_____

_____

_____

If I were to fast forward to the future, which decision would I regret the least and why?

_____

_____

_____

_____

_____

_____

_____

_____

_____

Thinking of the contribution I want to leave in this world, how does each decision allow me to make a difference?

_____

_____

_____

_____

_____

_____

_____

_____

How does each decision allow me to use my gifts, talents and passions to the maximum?

_____

_____

_____

_____

_____

_____

_____

_____

What is my intuition telling me?

_____

_____

_____

_____

_____

_____

_____

_____

_____

Removing ego, removing fear of failure, removing fear of the unknown, which decision stands out when I look strictly through the lens of love, for myself, my future self, and my overall calling?

_____

_____

_____

_____

_____

_____

_____

_____

_____

Questions to Reflect on when you Feel Stuck

Feeling stuck is something that happens to all of us at some point in our lives. When this feeling happens, pause for a moment, and revisit your purpose. Lean into this feeling of being stuck and understand what it might be trying to teach you. After this reflection and potential redirection, I invite you to then focus on the small steps you can take that will help you move in the right direction.

Searching Within

Focusing on my 'why', what motivates me to do what I do in all areas of my life?

_____

_____

_____

_____

_____

_____

_____

_____

_____

Now, in the area I am feeling stuck, why did I start this work in the first place? What was my motivation?

_____

_____

_____

_____

_____

_____

_____

_____

How will accomplishing these goals help the world to be a better place?

_____

_____

_____

_____

_____

_____

_____

_____

_____

Does this area still align with my overall 'why' statement and life purpose? If so, write down all the ways it still aligns. If not, is there anything that could be done differently in order to create this alignment?

_____

_____

_____

_____

_____

_____

_____

_____

Is there a negative belief I have about myself that is holding me back? What story do I tell myself that might be limiting me?

_____

_____

_____

_____

_____

_____

_____

_____

Evaluating a Specific Obstacle on your Path

Although there is an obstacle in my way, once this is cleared, is my path moving in a positive and favorable direction? If no, what options can I consider in order to steer my path in that direction?

_____

_____

_____

_____

_____

_____

_____

_____

_____

Once I get past this obstacle, is the outcome still as desirable as originally anticipated? If no, what has changed? How can I adjust what I can control in light of this?

_____

_____

_____

_____

_____

_____

_____

_____

_____

What have I learned by going through this experience?

_____

_____

_____

_____

_____

_____

_____

_____

_____

What <u>experience</u> can I bring to help me solve this obstacle?

_____

_____

_____

_____

_____

_____

_____

_____

What <u>skills</u> can I bring to help me solve this obstacle?

_____

_____

_____

_____

_____

_____

_____

_____

What can <u>my network</u> bring me to help me solve this obstacle?

_____

_____

_____

_____

_____

_____

_____

_____

_____

What does my end result look like? How will I feel?

_____

_____

_____

_____

_____

_____

_____

_____

_____

Famous Quotes and Inspiration

"Tell me what it is you plan to do with your one wild and precious life?"
Mary Oliver

_____

_____

_____

_____

_____

_____

_____

_____

_____

"Life's most persistent and urgent question is, 'What are you doing for others?' Martin Luther King Jr.

"What is something that I can do to add value to the world today?" Tony
Robbins

"For true success ask yourself these four questions: Why? Why not?
Why not me? Why not now?" Jimmy Dean

Section 4: Adversity

"We don't develop courage by being happy every day. We develop it by surviving difficult times and challenging adversity." Barbara De Angelis

"Opportunities to find deeper powers within ourselves come when life seems most challenging." Joseph Campbell

With some of life's most beautiful moments come hardship, heartache, and pain. And what we know for certain is that no one is a stranger to this, as everyone will have to go through a difficult situation at some point in their lives. The difference in outcome will be in how you choose to overcome these situations. This next section of questions is intended to help you reframe some of life's toughest moments through the lens of love, courage, and hope. These questions will help you get through the ups and downs of this beautiful journey we call life.

Questions for Self-love in times of Adversity

Being honest with myself, what do I feel right now? *Be honest and real with yourself and use this section to get everything out of your head. Use additional paper if necessary.*

_____

_____

_____

_____

_____

_____

_____

_____

- What clarity did I gain by writing everything out and acknowledging my feelings in the above question?

_____

_____

_____

_____

_____

_____

_____

_____

How can I be kinder to myself through this experience? What might I need that I am currently not giving myself?

_____

_____

_____

_____

_____

_____

_____

_____

Alongside everything that is happening in my life, what am I really proud of myself for at this moment? What can I pause and take a moment to celebrate during my adversity?

_____

_____

_____

_____

_____

_____

_____

_____

_____

What are five things I love about myself, as I go through this adversity?

_____

_____

_____

_____

_____

_____

_____

What can I do today that will make tomorrow or the next week easier?

_____

_____

_____

_____

_____

_____

_____

What might my intuition be telling me through this experience?

_____

_____

_____

_____

_____

_____

_____

_____

How is God/the universe fully guiding me through this time?

_____

_____

_____

_____

_____

_____

_____

_____

If a coach was here to give me an encouraging talk and build me up,
what would s/he say?

_____

_____

_____

_____

_____

_____

_____

_____

Are there specific moments throughout the day that are triggers for me
where I end up going to a sad place? How can I anticipate those and give
myself love through those hard moments?

_____

_____

_____

_____

_____

_____

_____

_____

_____

Knowing I have specific triggers or items that can upset me, how can I reframe them and see them as a reminder of love or a growth opportunity when they come up during the day? How can I change the story I tell myself in those moments to a story of love and gratitude?

_____

_____

_____

_____

_____

_____

_____

_____

Knowing that this too shall pass, where is there hope in this situation? How can I carry hope with me throughout my day?

_____

_____

_____

_____

_____

_____

_____

How can I apply my values to this situation?

_____
_____
_____
_____
_____
_____
_____
_____

How can I be love in this situation, for myself and for others?

_____
_____
_____
_____
_____
_____
_____

When I tell others about this situation in the future, how do I want to recount my growth and say I overcame this adversity?

_____
_____
_____
_____
_____
_____
_____

What have I not said to anyone else, or even myself, that I really need to vent? If I am being completely honest about my feelings, what do I need to get off my chest?

_____

_____

_____

_____

_____

_____

_____

What are three to five negative emotions or memories I am holding onto through this?

_____

_____

_____

_____

_____

_____

_____

_____

- How can I release these emotions and set them free, in turn setting myself free from them?

_____

_____

_____

_____

_____

_____

_____

_____

- Is there an opportunity to practice forgiveness or grace?

_____

_____

_____

_____

_____

_____

_____

_____

_____

- Knowing I am responsible for how I react to these emotions, how can I empower myself by and reframe the story?

_____

_____

_____

_____

_____

_____

_____

_____

_____

Questions for Clarity, Learning, and Growth

What lessons have I already learned from this situation?

_____

_____

_____

_____

_____

_____

_____

_____

_____

Is this circumstance teaching me to redirect my life or focus in any way?

_____

_____

_____

_____

_____

_____

_____

_____

How can this turn into a positive story or a life lesson/growth story?

_____

_____

_____

_____

_____

_____

_____

_____

Knowing my life has been full of growth and learnings up to this point, what skills, life experience, or perspectives can I use to help me get through this?

_____

_____

_____

_____

_____

_____

_____

_____

_____

Do I know any role models or people I admire that have gone through something similar? What could I learn from them?

_____

_____

_____

_____

_____

_____

_____

_____

Are there any patterns that I can recognize in myself that I often repeat in similar situations? Is this an opportunity for me to grow and change my usual behavior?

_____

_____

_____

_____

_____

_____

_____

_____

Where am I making decisions in my life based out of fear versus love?
How can I make decisions today based on love instead of fear?

_____

_____

_____

_____

_____

_____

_____

_____

_____

How can I lean into this situation and allow it to help me grow?

_____

_____

_____

_____

_____

_____

_____

_____

What is my intention through this? Are there any areas where my
intention has been misaligned with my values?

_____

_____

_____

_____

_____

_____

_____

_____

_____

How can I use this situation to strengthen me to become a strong, better version of myself?

_____

_____

_____

_____

_____

_____

_____

_____

If I was a neutral third party, what advice would I give myself at this moment?

_____

_____

_____

_____

_____

_____

_____

_____

In my life right now, what are five things that are going well? How can I express gratitude in these areas?

_____

_____

_____

_____

_____

_____

_____

_____

_____

_____

"What are you reacting to? Ask yourself that question every moment of every day when your peace is disturbed" Kenneth Wapnick

_____

_____

_____

_____

_____

_____

_____

_____

Questions for when you are Feeling Hopeless

Sitting with my emotions and feelings, what do I feel? What am I mad about? What am I sad about? What am I hurt about? *Be honest with yourself and allow yourself to feel the adversity you are going through. Use this question to acknowledge the pain you are feeling.*

_____

_____

_____

_____

_____

_____

_____

_____

How can I support and love myself right now?

_____

_____

_____

_____

_____

_____

_____

_____

Although I am feeling hopeless, where is there still hope in my life? Why am I thankful for this?

_____

_____

_____

_____

_____

_____

_____

_____

_____

What are five things that are still beautiful in this world?

_____

_____

_____

_____

_____

_____

_____

_____

_____

What in this moment am I still thankful for?

_____

_____

_____

_____

_____

_____

_____

_____

How can I use this experience to help others or contribute to others?

_____

_____

_____

_____

_____

_____

_____

_____

How will this experience make me stronger and more resilient?

_____

_____

_____

_____

_____

_____

_____

_____

_____

What is the largest opportunity for love or abundance in this situation?

_____

_____

_____

_____

_____

_____

_____

_____

_____

Who are 1-5 people that love me unconditionally? How can I lean into this love and use it to make me stronger during this time of feeling hopeless?

_____

_____

_____

_____

_____

_____

_____

_____

Who might need me to be my best and brightest? How can I let that motivate me to show up as my best self?

_____

_____

_____

_____

_____

_____

_____

_____

_____

What are five things I am proud of myself for, in any area of my life?

_____

_____

_____

_____

_____

_____

_____

If I were to write a note to myself in the future, after I have gone through this situation, what would I say to myself?

_____

_____

_____

_____

_____

_____

_____

_____

Forgiveness, Compassion, and Healing

"To forgive is to set a prisoner free and discover that the prisoner was you."
Lewis B. Smedes

The journey to forgiveness can be a hard, reflective path. This path is ultimately one that will set you free in the end. These questions evaluate a specific person or situation that hurt you and you are finding it hard to let it go. Walkthrough these questions with a compassionate heart, first and foremost, for yourself.

If I were to write this person or situation a letter, to get everything I am angry and hurt about off my chest, what would I say?

_____

_____

_____

_____

_____

_____

_____

_____

_____

Oftentimes our inability to forgive comes from us holding on to our own idea of the way the future was 'supposed to be'. We are angry with someone or something that changed the outcome of our lives in a way we didn't want. The first step of healing can often be to acknowledge that although this, unfortunately, happened to you, it is your responsibility to accept, heal, and grow from it.

If this rings true to me, how can I change the story I tell myself around this event, seeing it as something that was meant to cross my path in order to help me grow and give me strength? How would my story change to one of compassion and love, and empowerment for healing? *Write your story to one that will inspire someone going through exactly what you are going through.*

_____

_____

_____

_____

_____

_____

_____

_____

How have I grown from this event? How can going through this event teach me something and help me become a stronger and better person?

_____

_____

_____

_____

_____

_____

_____

_____

What are five affirmations I can tell myself that would help me heal?

_____

_____

_____

_____

_____

_____

_____

_____

_____

How might these events shape my future? How can I make it a positive story instead of a victim story in my future?

_____

_____

_____

_____

_____

_____

_____

_____

_____

What do I gain from holding onto this? *Be honest with yourself. Some people find their identity in their pain, or find they get special attention from their pain. See if there is anything that is causing you to not actually want to release this hurt and anger*

_____

_____

_____

_____

_____

_____

_____

_____

When I release this burden of anger and hurt, how can I use this freed up energy and space to love myself more?

_____

_____

_____

_____

_____

_____

_____

_____

_____

How can I change my past and story to see myself as a hero instead of a victim through this event?

_____

_____

_____

_____

_____

_____

_____

_____

What am I proud of myself for in overcoming this?

_____

_____

_____

_____

_____

_____

_____

What have been some unexpected blessings or learnings from this, if any?

_____

_____

_____

_____

_____

_____

_____

_____

_____

Now taking my attention fully off the past, what direction do I fully
want to take my life? How can I ensure I redirect my energy here instead
of reliving the past?

_____

_____

_____

_____

_____

_____

_____

_____

_____

Epilogue

As you worked through the reflection questions in this book, I hope you felt a sense of pride and love for yourself. You have chosen to invest in the most important journey you will ever take; one of healing and growth. I hope you noticed your thought pattern gradually shift to one of self-love, acceptance, optimism, and peace.

As I have learned through my own journey, the beauty of this process is that it never ends; growth and healing are continuous journeys. Knowing that, I invite you to continue this journey at www.questionstochangeyourlife.com and on social media (@questionstochangeyourlife). There you will find resources, a community, and an opportunity to share your own story and learnings with like-minded people. If you found this book helped you, I invite you to recommend it to a friend. Together, we will change the world by first examining, changing, and healing ourselves. Thank you for your commitment to growth and healing.

Afterword

A note from the Author, continuing the story from the Preface...

My mother ended up passing away after a six month battle with cancer. She was the light of every room she was in and we will miss her dearly. I didn't know what to expect in terms of the grief that would follow. Although I had an open mind, knowing grief sometimes has a unique journey of its own. I accepted that I was in a grieving phase of my life. Oftentimes we run and hide from hard emotions and pain, for valid reasons. I am learning the value of sitting with these raw, human emotions, acknowledging them, and letting myself feel them. Grief, pain, and adversity are some of life's best teachers and are an important part of everyone's story. Learning to accept this part of my story, and even appreciate some of their moments has allowed love, forgiveness, and compassion to show up in some of the most special ways. I'm proud that I can look at adversity in my life and choose to see love, compassion, gratitude, and guidance from a higher power. I know this is from years of reframing the questions I ask myself and choosing to find it in every situation.

I wanted to leave you with a piece of my story to remind you that life has an interesting way of throwing all kinds of curves at us. Everyone has learning, growth, and adversity to face in their lifetime. What I know for certain is that everything you need to succeed is within you; if we shift our thoughts, as this book has helped us do, we can choose to see the beauty and hope that life really holds.

As you continue to travel through your journey, please know that the community and I are always here to support you. I look forward to connecting and hearing some of your stories as I have shared mine with you. Join me at www.questionstochangeyourlife.com, or connect with me on social media (@Questionstochangeyourlife). I look forward to meeting you there.

With love,

Melissa Lashyn

References

Gratitude references:

Emmons, R. A., & McCullough, M. E. (2003). Counting blessings versus burdens: An experimental investigation of gratitude and subjective well-being in daily life. *Journal of Personality and Social Psychology*, 84(2), 377–389. https://doi.org/10.1037/0022-3514.84.2.377

Wood, A. M., Maltby, J., Gillett, R., Linley, A., Joseph, S. (2008). The role of gratitude in the development of social support, stress, and depression: Two longitudinal studies. *Journal of Research in Personality*, 48(4), 854-871. https://doi.org/10.1016/j.jrp.2007.11.003

Algoe, S. B., Haidt, J., & Gable, S. L. (2008). Beyond reciprocity: Gratitude and relationships in everyday life. *Emotion*, 8(3), 425–429. https://doi.org/10.1037/1528-3542.8.3.425

About the Author

Melissa Lashyn is motivated by helping people live to their fullest potential. After losing her mother to cancer, she was inspired to create a book that would help people build a strong mindset for both living out their potential and facing any adversity that may come their way.

Melissa resides in Alberta, Canada and spends much of her free time hiking and cross-country skiing in the mountains.

CPSIA information can be obtained
at www.ICGtesting.com
Printed in the USA
LVHW041101180920
666471LV00002B/343